HIGH RISK

U.S. PRESIDENTS WHO WERE KILLED IN OFFICE

CHILDREN'S GOVERNMENT BOOKS

UNIVERSAL POLITICS

POLITICS & SOCIAL SCIENCES

Speedy Publishing LLC

40 E. Main St. #1156

Newark, DE 19711

www.speedypublishing.com

Copyright 2017

Some of the wisest and most able people in the United States have run for high office and have served as President. Four have them have been killed, and many more have been attacked, while they served their country. Read on and learn about the dangers of being president.

MR· PRESIDENT

The most powerful political job in the United States, and perhaps in the whole world, is that of President. The President not only sets the direction of government policy at home and in regard to other countries, he is also the commander-in-chief of the largest and most powerful military force in the world.

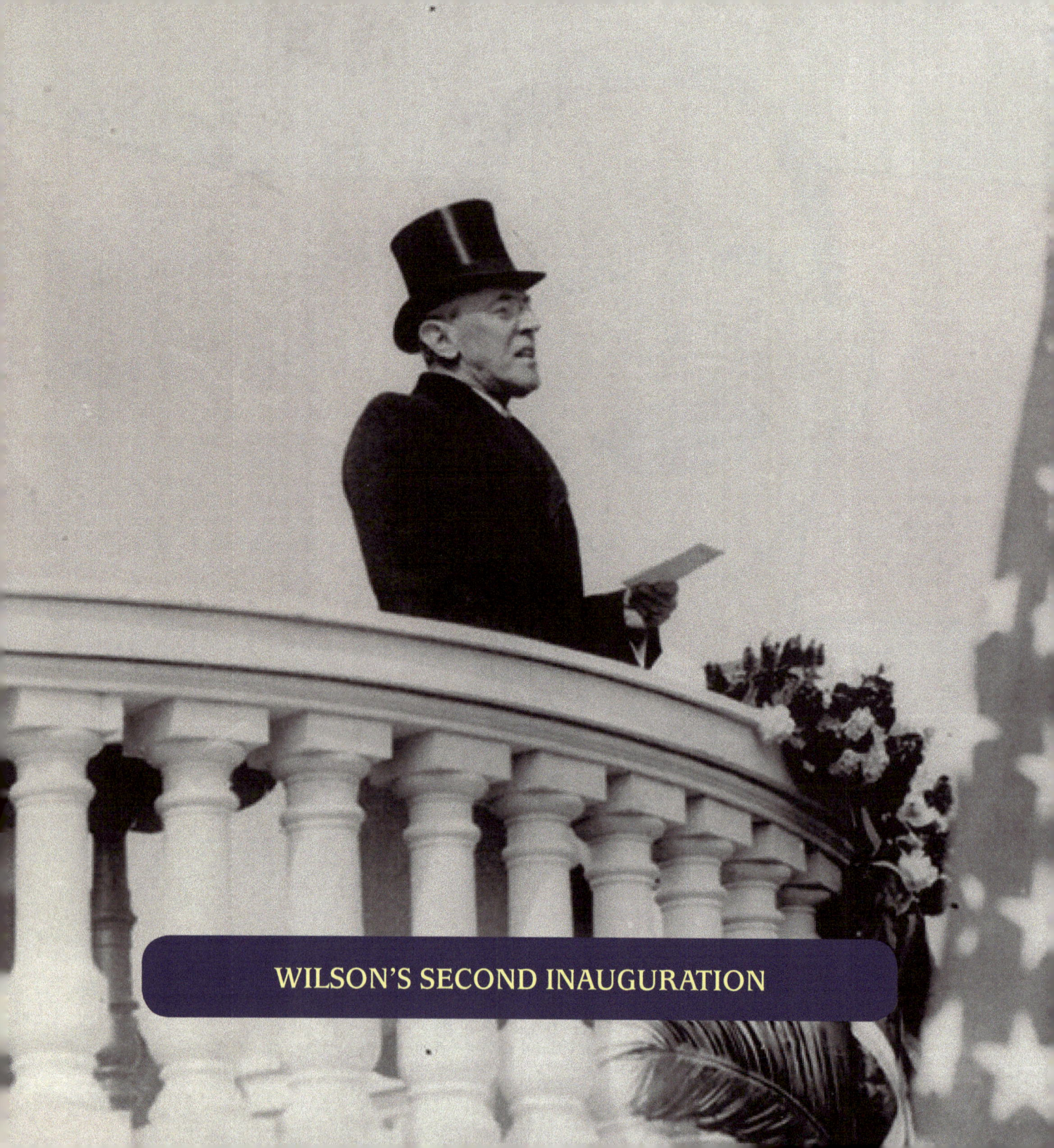

WILSON'S SECOND INAUGURATION

Being the top of the heap also makes the president a tempting target for people of many types. Some people don't like what the president stands for or what the country is doing under his orders. Some people focus on the president even though the source of the problems in their lives comes from somewhere else altogether.

Most of those upset about the president never do more than complain to their friends about him, posting something threatening on social media, or sending hate mail. But some take more drastic action to remove the president—and sometimes they succeed.

ABRAHAM LINCOLN

President Abraham Lincoln was shot and killed less than a week after the end of the American Civil War, in April, 1865. His assassin was John Wilkes Booth, a sympathizer of the defeated Confederate side in the war. Booth evidently thought that killing the U.S. president would somehow change the outcome of the war. The attack on the president was part of a plot to kill several key leaders of the federal government.

ABRAHAM LINCOLN

L incoln was attending a play when Booth entered the box where he was sitting and shot the president in the head with a small pistol. Lincoln died the next day despite desperate attempts to save his life.

Booth was shot and killed about two weeks later.
Vice President Andrew Johnson, who had also
been targeted for killing, became president.

JAMES A. GARFIELD

President Garfield arrived in Washington, D.C. from Baltimore, Maryland by train on July 2, 1881, only four months after becoming president. Charles Guiteau, who had a persecution complex and some sort of mental disorder, shot the president twice from behind. Despite expert medical aid, President Garfield never recovered from his wounds, which became infected.

JAMES A. GARFIELD

He suffered for eleven weeks before dying on September 19. Vice President Chester Arthur became president.

Guiteau was tried for murder, found guilty, and executed.

GUITEAU HOLDING A GUN AND A NOTE

WILLIAM MCKINLEY

President McKinley was shot in Buffalo, New York on the afternoon of September 6, 1901. Leon Czolgosz, who opposed any form of organized government, shot the president twice from short range. He died a week later, and Vice President Theodore Roosevelt became president.

WILLIAM MCKINLEY

Czolgosz was tried and found guilty in a rushed trial, and was executed October 29.

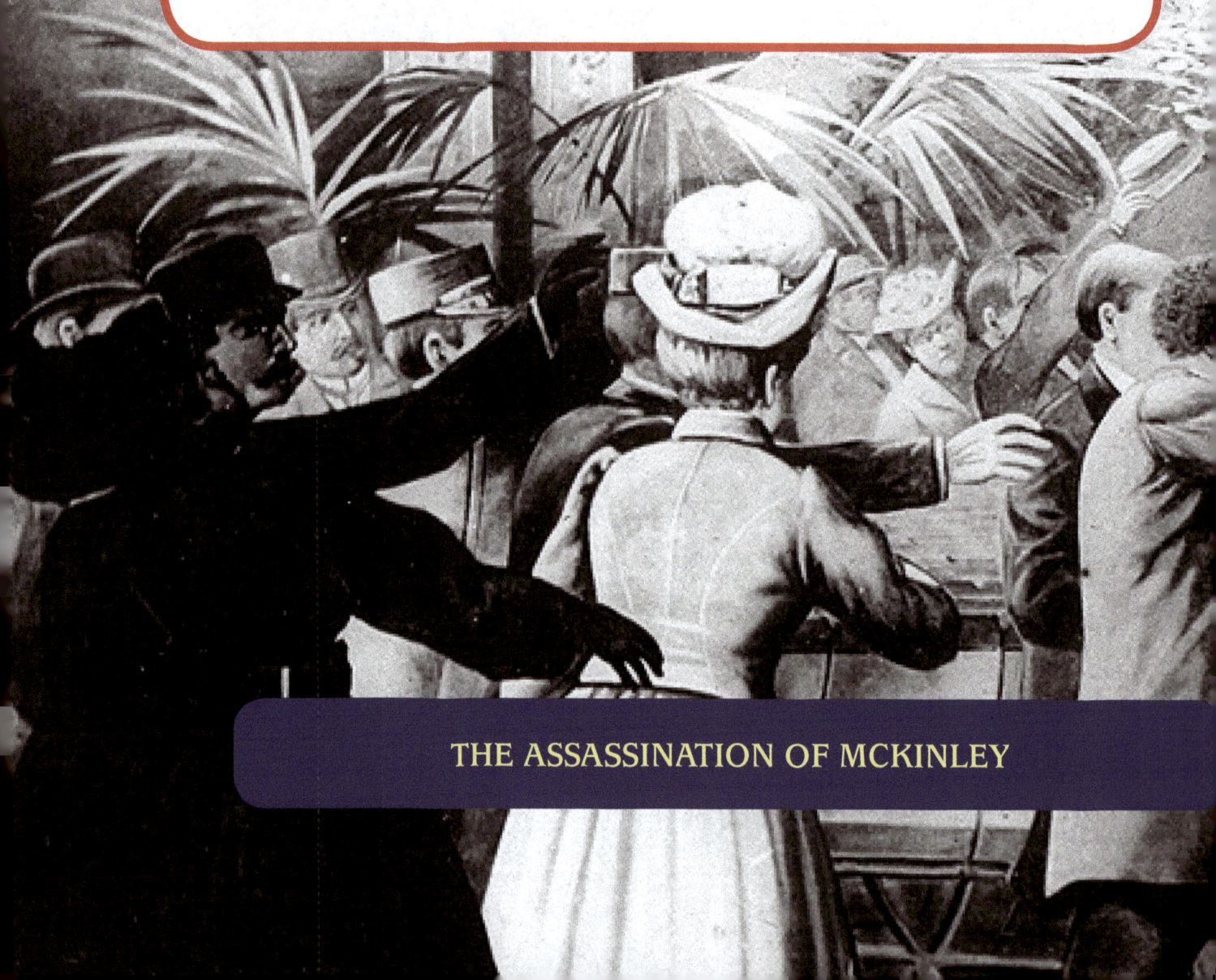

THE ASSASSINATION OF MCKINLEY

From this point on, the United States Secret Service took on the job of protecting the presidents of the United States.

JOHN F. KENNEDY

President Kennedy was visiting Dallas, Texas November 22, 1963. He was traveling in a motorcade with his wife and John Connally, the governor of Texas. Lee Harvey Oswald, from an upper floor of a building near the route of travel, shot the president twice with a rifle. The president was dead within thirty minutes. Vice President Lyndon Baines Johnson became president.

JOHN F. KENNEDY

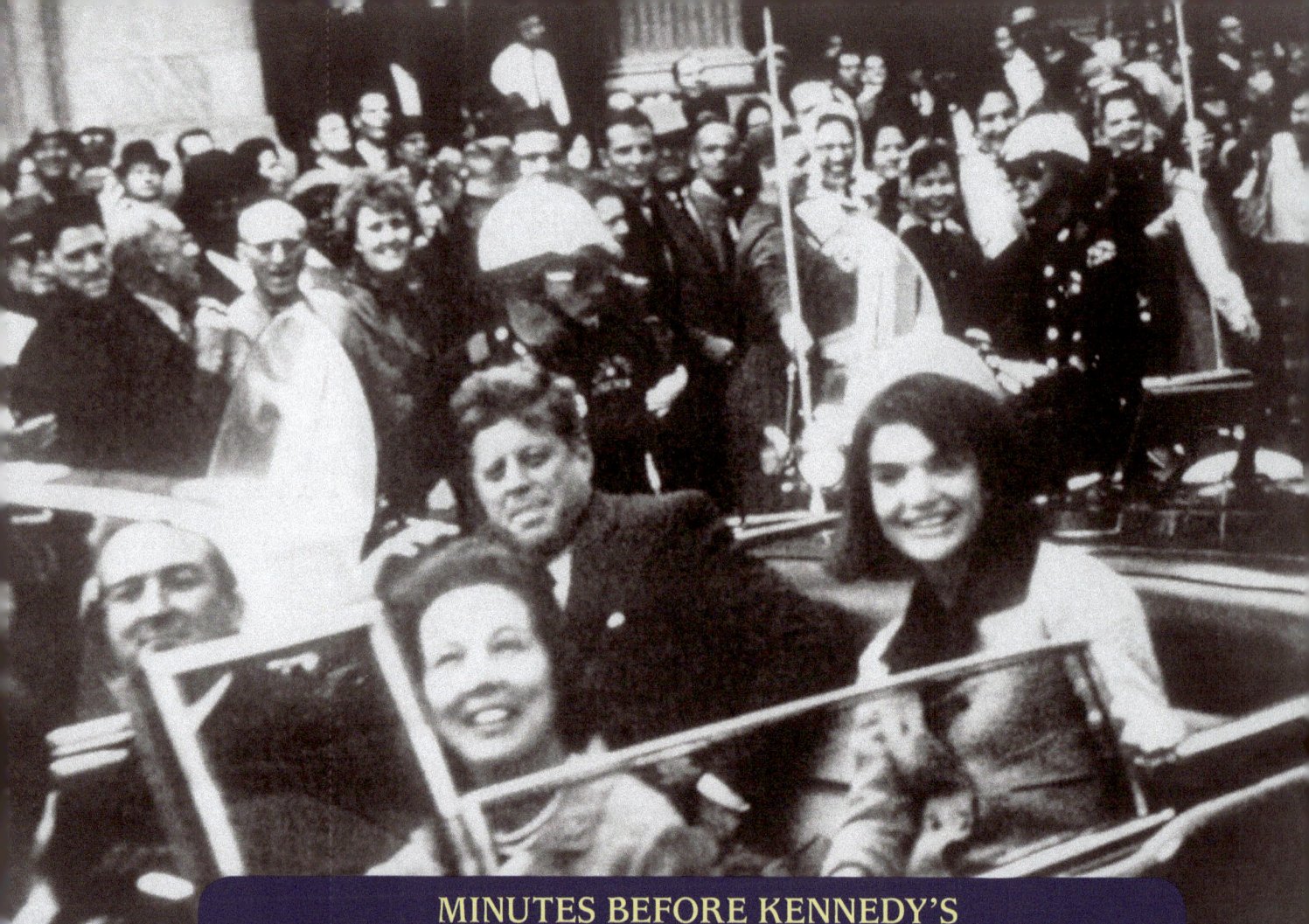

Oswald was arrested soon after. As police were transferring him to a jail, Oswald was shot and killed by a nightclub operator, Jack Ruby. It was never learned why Oswald attacked the president, and many conspiracy theories have grown up over the years about what "really" happened, and suggesting there may have been more than one gunman. Ruby was convicted of the murder of Oswald, sentenced to a life in prison, and died four years later in captivity.

CLOSE ESCAPES

This list of four assassinated presidents is terrible, but it could be much longer! Here are some other attacks on U.S. presidents that almost worked. Some were frustrated by bad luck and some by quick action by those around the president.

ANDREW JACKSON

ANDREW JACKSON

On January 30, 1835, a man tried to shoot President Jackson, but both his pistols failed. Jackson attacked the man with a walking stick, beating him to the ground.

ABRAHAM LINCOLN

In August of 1864, less than a year before he was killed, Lincoln was riding by himself from the White House to the Soldiers' Home hospital. Someone fired a rifle at him, knocking a hole in his hat.

WILLIAM HOWARD TAFT

WILLIAM HOWARD TAFT

Taft and Mexican president Porfirio Díaz were due to meet in Mexico in 1909, the first time a U.S. president would cross the border while in office. Thousands of security officers combined to try to keep both leaders safe. On the day of the meeting, October 16, a man with a pistol was arrested on the parade route.

THEODORE ROOSEVELT

Roosevelt, who had served most of two terms as president, left office in 1909. In October, 1912, he was running for election again at the head of the Progressive Party. He was in Milwaukee, Wisconsin, preparing to give a speech. The text of his speech was fifty pages long, and the manuscript was folded once and placed in his coat pocket along with his metal glasses case.

THEODORE ROOSEVELT

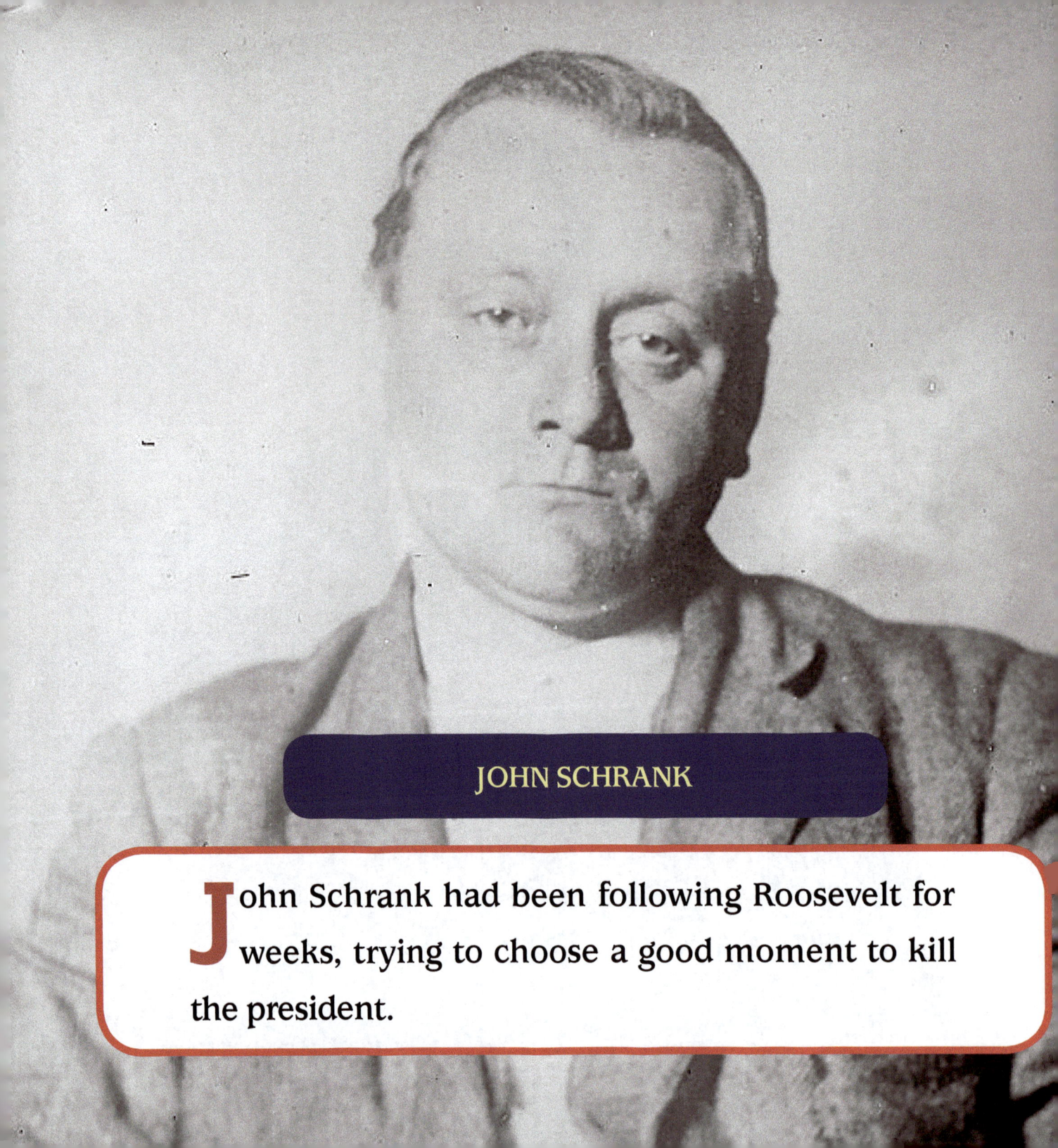

John Schrank had been following Roosevelt for weeks, trying to choose a good moment to kill the president.

On October 14, he shot Roosevelt in the chest. The thickness of the manuscript and the metal glasses case slowed down the bullet.

S chrank was captured right away. Amazingly, after concluding he was not going to die immediately, Roosevelt gave his speech with the bullet still in him! He then went to a local hospital.

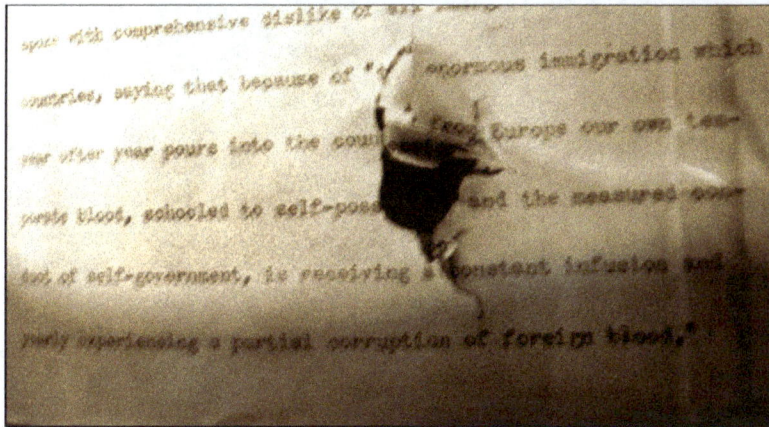

ASSISSINATION BULLET DAMAGE

Doctors decided not to try to remove the bullet, as it was awkwardly placed, and Roosevelt carried the bullet in his chest until his death in 1919, seven years later. It would be nice to report that Roosevelt won the election after that near-death experience, but he did not.

ROOSEVELT FUNERAL 1919

HERBERT HOOVER

HERBERT HOOVER

In South America in 1928, a group planned to blow up the train President Hoover was traveling in across Argentina. The police arrested a member of the group as he was about to plant the bomb, and foiled the plot.

FRANKLIN DELANO ROOSEVELT

Roosevelt was in Miami, Florida in February, 1933, just before his first inauguration as president. Giuseppe Zangara fired at the president's party, wounding five people and killing the mayor of Chicago. It is possible the intended target was the mayor and that the attack was related to gang activity in Illinois; in any case, Roosevelt was not hit.

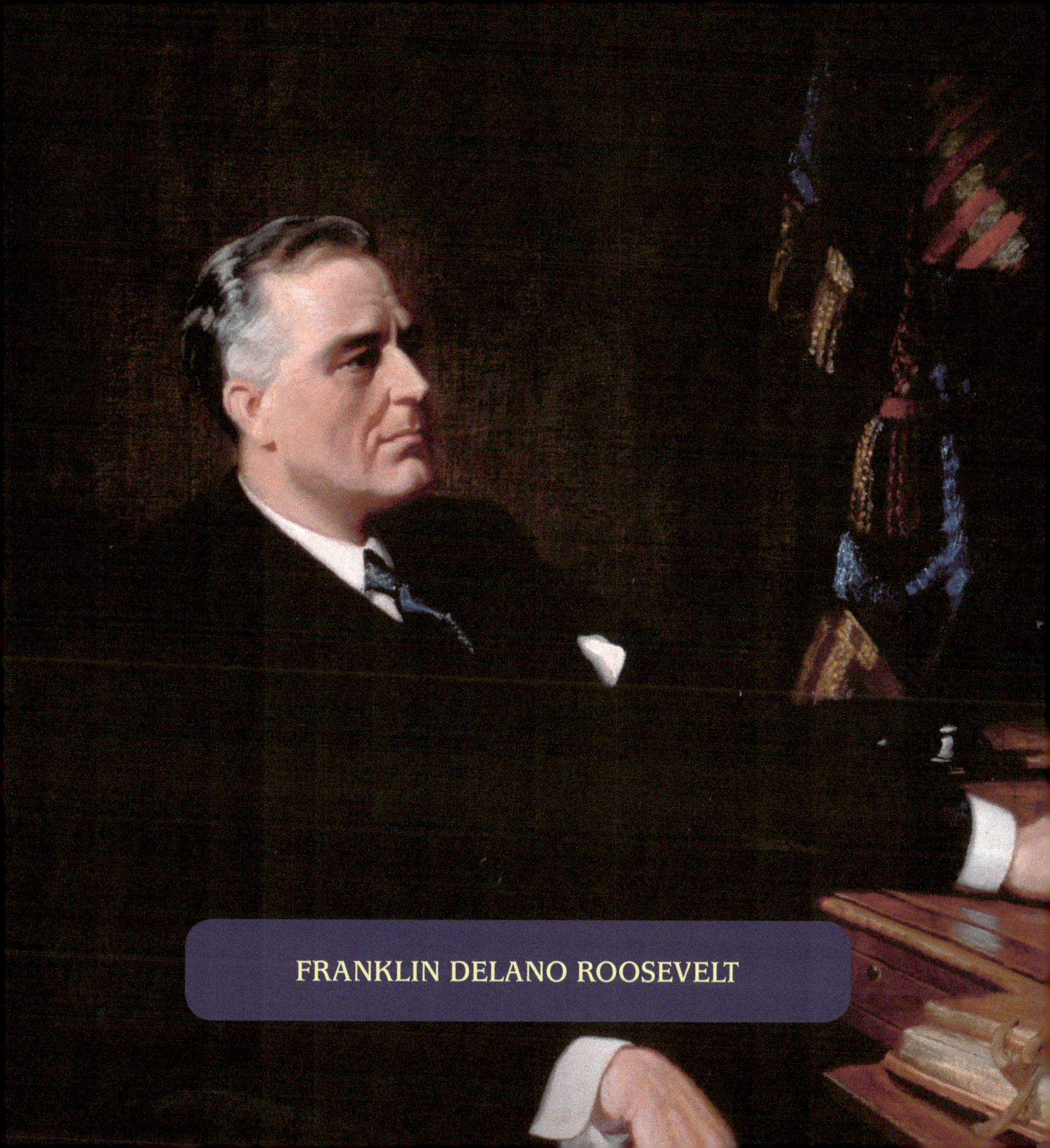

FRANKLIN DELANO ROOSEVELT

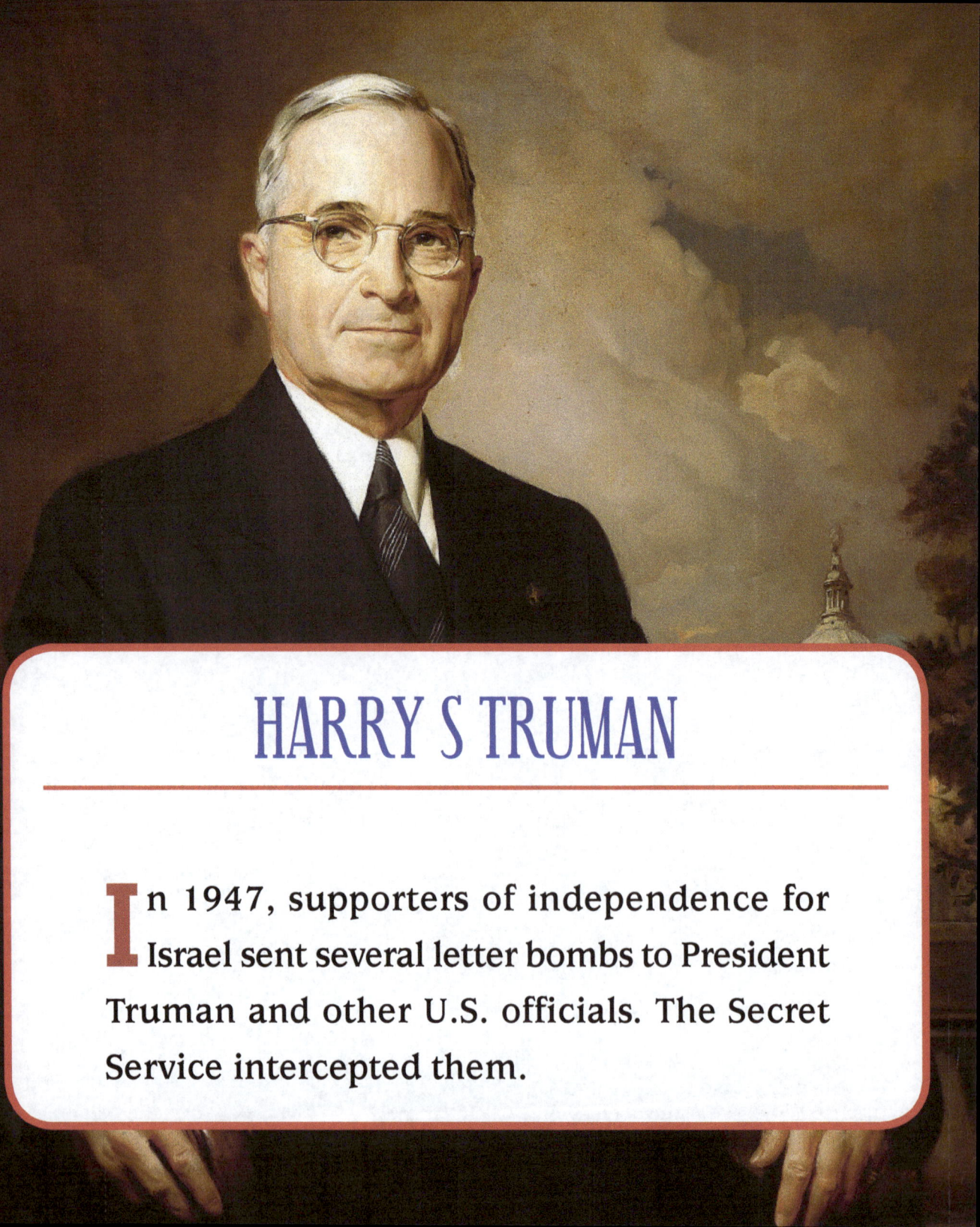

HARRY S TRUMAN

In 1947, supporters of independence for Israel sent several letter bombs to President Truman and other U.S. officials. The Secret Service intercepted them.

In 1950, supporters of Puerto Rican independence attacked Truman's residence, wounding several officers. Truman was not hurt.

MILITARY POLICE STAND GUARD IN FRONT
OF THE "LITTLE WHITE HOUSE"

GERALD FORD

Supporters of cult leader and mass-murderer Charles Manson twice tried to kill President Ford in 1975. Once the gun failed to fire, and the second time the bullet missed its intended target.

GERALD FORD

RONALD REAGAN

RONALD REAGAN

President Reagan gave a speech at a hotel in Washington, D.C. in 1981. As he went to his car, John Hinckley, Jr. shot the president and three other people. Reagan was saved by emergency surgery and returned to office within a few weeks.

BILL CLINTON

In 1994, a man fired about 30 rounds from a semi-automatic rifle at a group of men standing outside the White House, thinking President Clinton was one of them (he was actually inside).

In 1996 the Secret Service foiled a bomb plot aimed at President Clinton by terrorist leader Osama bin Laden, the man behind the 9/11 attacks on the United States in 2001.

GEORGE W. BUSH

GEORGE W. BUSH

In February, 2001, a man fired a number of shots at the White House, but did not hit the president.

In 2005, President Bush was in the country of Georgia, a former part of the Soviet Union. While he was giving a speech in Freedom Square in the capital, Tbilisi, someone threw a hand grenade toward where Bush was speaking.

The grenade's pin had been pulled and it was wrapped in a cloth so people would not know what it was, but the cloth prevented the safety lever from moving and the grenade did not explode.

BARACK OBAMA

BARACK OBAMA

In November, 2011, while President Obama was in the White House, a man who believe that he was Jesus Christ and the president was an agent of the devil fired at the White House several times. The bullets broke a window, but nobody was hit.

LIVE BRAVELY

Although you rarely know the day you will die, you can be sure that day will eventually come. The point of your life is how you live it while you can, not how long you stretch it out. All these men who served as president did so at considerable sacrifice, for the good of their country and to put forward programs in which they believed.

STAND BRAVELY FOR WHAT YOU BELIEVE

What will you stand bravely for in your life? You may not know until a crisis comes. Read about some people who cared more about what they believed in than in preserving or lengthening their own lives in these Baby Professor books: Brave Women of World War II, A Rich Man in Poor Clothes: The Story of St. Francis of Assisi, and Hitler's Bold Challengers.

Visit

UNIVERSAL POLITICS
✦ POLITICS & SOCIAL SCIENCES ✦

www.UniversalPolitics.com

to download Free Universal Politics eBooks
and view our catalog of new and exciting
Children's Books

Milton Keynes UK
Ingram Content Group UK Ltd.
UKHW051217040924
447642UK00021B/68

9 798869 413888